NEW JERSEY PORTRAITS 3

Dorothea L. Dix and the Politics of Institutional Reform

OCEAN COUNTY COLLEGE
LEARNING RESOURCES CENTER
TOMS RIVER, N.J. 08753

FREDERICK M. HERRMANN

New Jersey Historical Commission

For copies, write to the
New Jersey Historical Commission
113 W. State St., CN 520
Trenton, NJ 08625
© 1981 by the New Jersey Historical Commission
All rights reserved
Printed in the United States of America

Designed by Peggy Lewis and
Nancy H. Dallaire
Illustrations
Photos on cover and pages 4, 13, 30 courtesy
Trenton Psychiatric Hospital
Photo on page 20 courtesy
New Jersey Reference Section
New Jersey State Library

Library of Congress Cataloging in Publication Data

Herrmann, Frederick M 1947-
Dorothea L. Dix and the politics of institutional reform.

(New Jersey portraits ; 3)
Bibliography: p.
1. Dix, Dorothea Lynde, 1802-1887. 2. Social reformers—United States—Biography. I. New Jersey Historical Commission. II. Title. III. Series.
HV28.D6H47   362.2'1'0924 [B]   80-20051
ISBN 0-89743-051-4   ISSN 0162-8577

I come to ask *justice* of the Legislature of New Jersey, for those who, in the providence of God, are incapable of pleading their own cause, and of claiming redress for their own grievances. Be patient with me—it is for your own citizens I plead; it is for helpless, friendless men and women, in your very midst, I ask succour—into whose broken minds hope and consolation find no entrance—the foul air of whose dreary cells still oppresses my breath—the clanking of whose heavy chains still sounds upon my ear. Have pity upon them! have pity upon them!

Dorothea L. Dix, Memorial to the New Jersey Legislature, Journal of the Proceedings of the . . . Senate of the State of New Jersey, *January 23, 1845, p. 176.*

Dorothea Lynde Dix.

Social reformers of the nineteenth century can be understood only by comprehending the surroundings in which they functioned. The Industrial Revolution profoundly transformed the economy, social structure and political institutions of American society. It involved a great increase in knowledge and a widespread diffusion of learning. The rate of urbanization advanced, social and geographic mobility increased, labor became more specialized, immigrants rapidly grew in number, subsistence farming shifted to commercial agriculture, and the level of technological development rose. An urban-industrial society emerged in which formal, public institutions performed more and more of the functions previously discharged by the church, family and local community. These traditional institutions could no longer adequately deal with the problems of an increasingly complex society. Thus, new and specialized structures of state government began to carry out various functions deemed vital to the welfare of the American people.

Within this context, Dorothea Lynde Dix (1802–1887) attained an international reputation as a crusader for the institutional treatment and care of the mentally ill. She was also known as the major organizer of nursing care during the Civil War. Her labors for the insane contributed to the evolution of elaborate government structures that performed services previously provided in the private or local domain. In a sense, Dix's career may be understood as a chapter in the institutionalizing of state government that occurred in response to industrialization during the nineteenth century. Paradoxically, however, she conceived of herself as a social reformer obeying a religious imperative and perfecting a traditional and familiar society, not as an innovator of institutional structures. Acting only as a devout Unitarian seeking to implement her faith, Dix unconsciously participated in the transforming of a homogeneous and rural society with traditional values into a complex, urban-industrial society dominated by the modern state.[1]

Dorothea Dix's parentage and early life offered few clues to her destiny as the nineteenth century's most famous and influential psychiatric reformer. Her father, Joseph Dix, married Mary Bigelow, an impoverished woman eighteen years his senior, against his family's wishes. As punishment, Dr. Elijah Dix, Dorothea's grandfather and an eminent Boston physician, compelled his wayward son to leave his studies at Harvard and settled him on a distant Maine farm on the outskirts of Hampden, six miles below Bangor. Here Dorothea was born on April 4, 1802, to an exiled father entrusted with securing settlers for his parents' considerable frontier property holdings.[2]

Intemperate and unstable in many of his ways, Joseph Dix soon tired of acting as a land agent. He left the Congregational faith of his ancestors and espoused what Madam Dix, Dorothea's grandmother, called "fanatical" Methodism.[3] Soon, he became a prolific author of religious literature and spent his time writing and publishing tracts of little theological benefit to the world and much financial detriment to his struggling family. Dorothea and her mother aided this enterprise by stitching the tracts and pasting them together. At the age of twelve, Dorothea rebelled against this irksome work and her father's peculiar traits, and she ran away from her home, then in Worcester, Massachusetts.[4]

Arriving in Boston, the young runaway took up residence with her grandmother. By 1814, Madam Dix, a fine example of the dignified, precise, conscientious New England gentlewoman of her generation, had been a widow for five years but she was still living in the family home, the Dix Mansion. If Dorothea had expected an indulgent grandparent and a home free of discipline, she soon discovered her error. Although Madam Dix loved her granddaughter, she placed duty above affection. Industry, economy, and especially thoroughness were the chief precepts of the elder Dix's religion, and she instilled these virtues into her ward with a vigorous and harsh discipline. A week of solitary confinement was a typical penalty for a lapse of duty. Little wonder that the social reformer recollected later in her life, "I never knew childhood."[5]

At fourteen, Dix returned to Worcester and opened a school for small children. She conducted classes in an unoccupied room of a public schoolhouse. Discipline was stern and inflexible almost to the extreme. She taught her charges the rudiments of reading and writing, as well as manners, customs, and sewing. Morals and religion were also a part of her curriculum. The school remained in existence for nearly three years.[6]

In 1819, Dix returned to her grandmother's mansion in Boston, where two years later she established a school for young girls that she conducted, interrupted only by intervals of ill health, until she was thirty-three. The instruction reflected her interests and emphasized astronomy and the natural sciences. She also taught mathematics, reading and writing, in addition to such handicrafts as sewing and lace making. She had hardly started this school for the rich and fortunate when she opened another in a room above the mansion's carriage house for the poor and destitute.[7]

Among her pupils were the children of the Reverend William Ellery Channing. As a member of his congregation, she came under the renowned Unitarian minister's influence, which greatly intensified her deep religious commitment. Dix's devoutness surfaced early in a literary career that paralleled her teaching duties in the 1820s and early 1830s. Many of her books, such as *Meditations for Private Hours,* dealt with religious subjects that embodied the ideals of duty, perfection, and Christian piety. She also published several works for children and books of romantic sentiment typical of the era.[8]

Dix accomplished much by lengthening her work day. Following a rigorous, self-imposed schedule, she always rose before daylight to read the Bible. After breakfast, she spent protracted hours in teaching, study, and writing. Long after others went to bed, she continued her work. Following Dix's schedule would have been a stern ordeal for a healthy person; it was especially difficult for one with a frail constitution. Very early she had manifested a tendency toward throat and pulmonary disorders. The strain of teaching and writing eventually aggravated these conditions, and in 1836 she suffered a complete nervous and physical collapse.[9]

Obliged to close her school, she sailed for Europe on April 22. She hoped to relax during the crossing, rest in England over the summer, spend the autumn in France, and winter in Italy. However, after arriving in Liverpool, she found her condition greatly weakened rather than improved. To her good fortune, the William Rathbone family offered her the hospitality of their residence outside the city. Rathbone was a wealthy merchant, a prominent Unitarian, and a friend of William Ellery Channing. Intending to stay for only a few weeks, Dix remained instead as an honored guest for eighteen months. She considered this period "as the jubilee of her life, the sunniest, the most restful, and the tenderest to her affections of her whole earthly experience."[10]

On April 29, 1837, Madam Dix died in her Boston mansion. Since Dorothea's health prevented her immediate return home, she did not arrive in New England to claim the substantial legacy her grandmother had bequeathed until autumn. The sum supported her for the rest of her life. She would never have to teach again. The fact that at her death Madam Dix endowed one of the greatest social activists in American history may well preserve her memory.[11]

Dix spent the four years following her return from England in 1837 in aimless drifting, the vision of a life of social service slowly evolving, but its form not yet clear. Then, in 1841, John T.G. Nichols, a young student at the Harvard Divinity School, asked her to recommend a teacher for a Sunday school class in the women's department of the East Cambridge House of Correction. Dix volunteered, and began her career as a social reformer.[12] If she had died before that moment, she would have been remembered, if at all, only as a self-sacrificing school teacher and a minor author of some contemporary fame.

On a bitterly cold March day after teaching her class of prisoners, Dix walked through the jail and talked with the convicts. Among them, she found a number of emotionally disturbed persons confined in a dreary, unsanitary, and unheated room. She asked the jailer why these sick people had no stove and she was told that, for them, a fire would be unsafe and that "lunatics" did not feel the cold.[13] Deeply touched by the suffering and neglect she observed, the newly-converted social activist determined to improve the living conditions of the prison's insane.

Enlisting the support of other philanthropists, including Charles Sumner and Samuel Gridley Howe, Dix inititiated an investigation of the conditions in the East Cambridge prison and fought the matter through the newspapers. When the local court ordered the cold quarters of the mentally ill to be heated, Dix won the first victory of her new career. Aroused by the thought that perhaps "enlightened and humane" East Cambridge was not the only place in Massachusetts in which the insane were neglected and mistreated, she embarked on a two-year investigation of all the state's jails and poorhouses to prepare a complete report on the plight of the mentally ill.[14]

The manner in which Dix found the mentally ill treated in the East Cambridge jail prevailed in the early nineteenth century. In fact, it was superior to their treatment in most parts of Massachusetts and the rest of the nation. Before the Civil War, the mentally ill were frequently housed with criminals, paupers, and vagrants; confined in boxlike, dark, and ill-ventilated cells; allowed few visitors, little clothing, and no furniture; and given the coarsest of food. At the slightest evidence of violence, they were chained to the walls of their cells with iron collars that permitted little movement, and they were fortunate to be allowed to lie down to sleep on filthy mattresses.[15] In 1840, the insane in the United States numbered 17,456 out of a total population of 17,069,453; but the country's fourteen hospitals for the mentally ill had a capacity of less than twenty-five hundred beds.[16] America's general neglect of the insane and its failure to distinguish between the criminal and the mentally ill can be attributed to ignorance, medical misconceptions, and a lack of social consciousness. Although Dix was by no means the first person to attack these problems, her work was fundamental to rectifying them.[17]

In January 1843, Dix completed her investigation of the

Bay State and presented her findings in the famous "Memorial to the Legislature of Massachusetts." It was the first of many similar documents. The memorial gave a highly detailed picture of the conditions in virtually every prison and almshouse in the state. She insisted that the commonwealth had a legal, moral, and humanitarian obligation toward its mentally ill.[18] Her facts were irrefutable and brought an instant reaction. The keepers of some of the institutions she had visited and certain legislators hurled charges of "sensational and slanderous lies." They accused Dix of being a sentimental idealist and a snooping, interfering woman. Nonetheless, with the aid of Horace Mann, Howe, and others, she convinced the legislature to provide additional facilities at the over-crowded Worcester State Lunatic Hospital.[19]

The success of her Massachusetts campaign was the beginning of Dix's nationwide effort for state-supported insane asylums. For the next three decades, she ceaselessly followed throughout the country a course of action similar to her Bay State activities. After arriving in a state, Dix meticulously surveyed the condition and treatment of its insane. Then she had her findings presented to the legislature, usually in the form of a long and emotional memorial. Seemingly conforming to mid-nineteenth century canons about the behavior of women, she never went before a legislature herself but chose influential men to plead her case publicly. From time to time, she boldly consulted a dozen or more male political leaders at her boarding house. Her letters and conversations provided them with material for speeches and the press.[20]

While surveying the prisons and almshouses of Massachusetts, Dix often crossed the borders of adjoining states to observe their provisions for the insane. She witnessed great misery in Rhode Island and New York. In the spring and summer of 1843, Dix turned her attention to Rhode Island and collected survey data to write a memorial, but she found that it would be unnecessary. Nicholas Brown, a distinguished merchant and a benefactor of Brown University, had bequeathed $30,000 for a Rhode Island asylum. However, since the sum was insufficient for the project, it was necessary to find other donors. Urged by Dix, Cyrus Butler, a penurious old bachelor who was notorious for his utter lack of generosity, agreed to give $40,000 if she could collect an equal sum from other sources.[21] By the end of 1845, Providence witnessed the opening of the Butler Hospital for the Insane.

In January 1844, Dix presented a memorial to the New York Legislature. It depicted the condition of the mentally ill in the state's county poorhouses. Based on a ten-week survey, the New York memorial recommended that four to six additional hospitals be built to care for the rapidly-increasing number of insane, who could not be handled properly in existing facilities. Unfortunately, Dix's proposals were taken lightly, and she was criticized for having an abrasive personality. In the end, she succeeded only in obtaining a larger appropriation for the Utica State Lunatic Asylum that had been founded in 1843.[22]

Having completed her work in Massachusetts, Rhode Island, and New York, Dix turned her attention to New Jersey. In her three previous crusades, she had been able only to enlarge on the work of others; however, in New Jersey, she succeeded in building an asylum. By 1844, the state had made some provisions for its blind and deaf, but it had neither private nor public facilities for the mentally ill. Local communities took responsibility for their care.[23] Thus, New Jersey gave Dix her first opportunity to found a mental institution. A review of the process and circumstances that led to the creation of Dix's first asylum may prove both rewarding and useful to grasping the nature and significance of her work nationally and the context in which she labored.

Antebellum New Jersey began its involvement in caring for the mentally ill in a cautious and experimental manner. Responding to rapid social and economic changes, the state's relief activities for the insane progressed from a reliance on local programs and a limited distribution of funds to state regulation and administration of benefits. New Jersey's developing urban-industrial society made communal, religious, and familial groupings ineffective in mental health care because of the proliferating mentally distressed and a growing working class with no ability to look after its sick. In a more complex era marked by the rise of urban poverty and factory work, the state government was forced to rely on specialized administrative procedures to dispense necessary aid. New Jersey residents were becoming conscious that existing institutions and methods were no longer adequate in a rapidly-changing society.²⁴

The establishment of the state's first mental hospital, however, was not the product of a systematic policy formulated through a careful analysis and evaluation of existing and future needs. New Jersey's political leaders acted only under goading from the state medical society and Dorothea Dix. In this period, the state government was engaged in anything but the uniform creation of policy. The legislature performed many of the administrative functions associated today with the executive branch of government. Rather than acting according to policies or large-scale plans, legislators of the era reacted to parochial requests for resources, privileges, and favors. Usually they met these demands with special enactments that kept legislative solutions largely isolated from each other.²⁵

New Jersey, like the federal government and other states, was unprepared to cope with the issues and the problems that arose with the basic social and economic changes of the nineteenth century. A major legacy of the American Revolution was a system of government that feared power and concomitantly distrusted a centralized bureaucracy headed by a strong chief executive. The state's authorities, consequently, were slow to secure and dispense public funds and to innovate policies. As a result, it was especially difficult, if not impossible, for New Jersey's elected officials to identify broad social demands and respond to them with adequate programs.²⁶

By the mid-1830s, the legislature was convinced that it had solved the problems of the state's indigent blind and deaf-mute citizens by making a small annual appropriation so that other states could educate and care for them. However, it was temporarily in a quandary about how to deal with the largest special group of poor—the mentally ill. Legislators could have sent them to out-of-state institutions, but did not because of their numbers and the unlikelihood that they could be rehabilitated or cured.²⁷ Industrialization, urbanization, the arrival of myriads of immigrant paupers, and a growing population combined during the 1840s to undermine New Jersey's reliance on traditional and formal mechanisms (such as the

Horace A. Buttolph, first superintendent (1847–1876) of the State Lunatic Asylum. Artist unknown. Photo by Peggy Lewis.

family, the church, and the local community) to alleviate the distress of the mentally ill. The undesirability of devolving their responsibility on neighboring states, the rising public indignation at the treatment of the insane in jails and poorhouses, the recent promise of medical science that curative treatment would work, and the need for the rationalization and centralization of welfare in a more complex society eventually led lawmakers to conclude that they must erect and administer a state mental hospital.[28]

Public attention was first directed to the problems of the insane and the necessity of providing a state-administered asylum for their treatment in the presidential address of Lyndon A. Smith of Newark before the state medical society in 1837. His colleagues supported the idea of a state mental institution, and, in 1839, the legislature appointed a joint committee to look into it.[29] Reporting on February 26, 1839, the committee lamented that it had too little time to consider the proposal to the extent that its importance demanded, and apologized for failing "to procure the statistical details necessary to enable the legislature to decide upon the necessity of the proposed institution." Consequently, the committee had no accurate way to ascertain the number, condition, or location of the state's mentally ill. However, by assuming that the ratio of insane to normal inhabitants was the same in New Jersey as in New England, it estimated that "there are now more than 800 citizens of this state . . . laboring under mental derangement." If only half this number required institutionalization, a mental hospital would be needed.[30]

It was unfortunate, the report continued, that no provision had been made, "either by public bounty or by private munificence," to remove the malady or alleviate the sufferings of the insane. Had not the state "in the spirit of enlightened humanity" stretched out its hand to aid the deaf and the blind? Why was there not a single line on the statute books to help "those whom Heaven has visited with its severest inflictions?" According to the committee, the real explanation lay in the fact that until the last few years most people regarded maniacs and lunatics as incurable. But now, it argued, when modern science showed that "mental maladies are as susceptible of cure as corporeal . . . the voice of awakened humanity demands that the effort should be made." Indeed, Jerseyans should make it their goal "to restore to usefulness those who are now utterly lost to the community."³¹

The committee informed the legislature that experience showed that a large majority of the emotionally disturbed placed in an asylum during the early stages of their disorder and subjected to humane and judicious treatment were restored to health. Yet, those whom society condemned to the "injudicious severity" of chains and a dungeon in a jail or a poorhouse became incurable. The poverty of a large proportion of these unfortunates made their support a burden to society. However, if the state would provide an asylum in which the patients could receive kind and cautious treatment, the committee believed that not only would the ill be relieved of their suffering, but the prospect of their restoration would increase greatly "without adding materially to the public burden." The report concluded with a resolution that called on the governor to appoint a commission to collect information about the number and condition of the state's insane and thereby determine if an asylum was necessary.³²

On February 26, 1840, the commission appointed by the governor to explore the possibilities of erecting a state asylum reported to the legislature. Four of its five members were doctors belonging to the New Jersey Medical Society. The commissioners divided the state among themselves, intending to visit the poorhouses and jails in which the mentally ill were kept and to inquire among local doctors and local officials. Two of the commissioners went to Massachusetts and surveyed the McLean Asylum at Charlestown, the State Lunatic Hospital at Worcester, and the General Hospital and State Penitentiary at Boston to gain additional information. The commissioners' incomplete and haphazard inquiry revealed 695 insane people living in New Jersey.³³

A few of the commissioners actually inspected the conditions under which the mentally afflicted lived, and their report included some horror stories. They found insane persons confined in jails either because they committed some flagrant outrage or because the community believed them to be dangerous when at large. Some localities kept their mentally ill confined for years, some of them *"in chains."* The commissioners specifically cited the counties of Gloucester, Cumberland, and Salem as well as the city of New Brunswick for such cruelty. Referring to a sick individual whose hands and legs had been chained to the floor in the Gloucester poorhouse, they stated that "it is highly probable that this man might be rendered useful to the community instead of being a burden, were he in a well-regulated institution."[34]

Marshalling their arguments, the commissioners wrote that a state hospital, which they strongly desired, would be "intended principally for that class of unfortunates, who for the want of such an establishment, are committed to jails, because the community is unsafe when they are at large." The emotionally ill had to be prevented from wandering at all hours, breaking into homes at night, and greatly disturbing "the repose of families." In many instances, the commissioners' report continued, "they pilfer for hunger—make violent assaults upon the defenseless—set fire to dwellings, and sometimes commit horrid murders." Of course, the security and order of society demanded their confinement, but to imprison them in county jails with felons and criminals only served to confirm their insanity and to eliminate their chances for recovery. The chief advantage of a state-run asylum was not only its provision for the custody of its patients but also its promise of their restoration.[35]

Every well-regulated mental hospital, the commissioners assured the legislators, placed its suffering patients in the care of persons who were trained and skilled in their treatment. Accordingly, such institutions could cure and discharge a large portion of their charges. Experience, they claimed, abundantly proved this assertion, especially in cases of recent insanity. Moreover, experience also showed that to incarcerate the insane or to confine them with chains and manacles in a poorhouse or in a family's home guaranteed that they would never recover. The commissioners concluded their approbation of a state mental facility by stating "it cannot be doubted that, with an appropriate treatment, one-half of at least all the lunatics, whose support must now continue to be a burden upon the

State while they live, might have been restored."[36]

The following year, 1841, a joint legislative committee reported its findings on the same issue. Using the statistics collected by the commissioners of 1840, the committee estimated that about two hundred indigent mentally ill had received support at public expense. It praised the commissioners' report for exposing the extreme wretchedness and suffering of the state's emotionally disturbed. After describing the brutal conditions under which mentally ill paupers existed in New Jersey, the joint committee called the legislature's attention to the necessity of a state-administered asylum as the best remedy for the sufferings of this "neglected class of our fellow beings."[37]

After briefly mentioning "the claims of humanity and justice," the committee based its appeal to the legislature for a state mental hospital on "the economy of such establishments." It calculated that the cost of supporting two hundred pauper lunatics was $1.75 a week each, or $18,200 a year for all of them. At the same time, the Ohio Lunatic Asylum operated for only $16,551.87, a sum significantly less "than that . . . paid by the citizens of New Jersey for the wretched maintenance of their insane poor" by local government. From the additional information the committee collected on the subject, it determined that after the completion of the asylum's main building an annual appropriation of $12,000 to $15,000 would sustain the institution housing all the state's insane paupers. Clearly then, an asylum would be the cheapest method of supporting the state's indigent insane.[38]

Based on its findings, the joint committee offered the legislature four resolutions. The first declared "that the confinement of insane persons in jails, with criminals, is subversive of all distinction between calamity and guilt and punishes the misfortune which it is the duty of society to relieve." In the second resolution, the committee stated that it was highly expedient that New Jersey provide a suitable institution for the comfort and relief of its insane poor because experience showed that "recent insanity, in most cases, is readily cured." Third, it resolved that an asylum be erected at state expense in a proper place selected by commissioners with the governor's approval.

Finally, the fourth resolution demanded a bill to embrace the ideas expressed in the previous three.[39]

After five years of serious contemplation and study, New Jersey was at last beginning to shed some of the traditional patterns of political behavior that militated against systematic policy formation and a strong role for the state. In collecting data, the state acknowledged that planning was a prerequisite for legislating. The various reports over the half-decade recognized that only direct state action could relieve the suffering of the insane and reduce the serious burden they placed on a newly industrialized society. Most significant, the investigating officials argued that the state aid the insane not only financially but also administratively. The state would actually control the daily operations of a welfare project, taking over local government's traditional role in this area.

The legislature, however, took no action. A committee appointed early in 1842 regretted that building a lunatic asylum had to be postponed but argued that "the present condition of monetary affairs" made any other course impossible.[40] An act of 1843 authorized the county boards of chosen freeholders to select "restorable pauper lunatics" to be taken either to a New York or Pennsylvania mental asylum and to be supported there.[41] Although the counties sent from sixty to eighty of their indigent insane to the institutions of New Jersey's two neighbors, the solution was inadequate because a much larger number stayed behind.[42]

In 1844, after seven years of futile efforts, New Jersey's movement for a state asylum for its insane appeared lost. But in the fall of that year, Dorothea Dix arrived in the state and revived the campaign for a public hospital. She planned to continue her previous work for the mentally ill by persuading the recalcitrant New Jersey Legislature to build the state's first mental institution. Her technique remained the same. She thoroughly surveyed the abominable condition of the state's insane, intending to use the results in a memorial that would appeal to the conscience and frugality of the legislature.[43]

Dix's odyssey into the world of New Jersey's insane is a tale about the evil capacities of mankind as gruesome and sad as anyone has ever witnessed and reported.[44] While traversing a considerable portion of the state in the last few months of 1844, she saw "scenes of almost incredible sufferings." In jails, poorhouses, and wandering at will over the countryside, the reformer found large numbers of the insane who were "left to exposures and sufferings, at once pitiable and revolting, and however in detail strongly expressed, incapable of being exaggerated." Her journey began in South Jersey in Salem County.

In the county's poorhouse, Dix uncovered particularly shocking conditions. She noted, besides several epileptics and persons of "infirm mind" kept there, eight insane inmates. One middle-aged woman had been unbalanced for seventeen years. Two of the patients were in chains, and one man, who had been mentally ill for nearly thirty years, had been out of his small apartment but " 'ten times . . . in nineteen years.' " He was justifiably considered dangerous. The poorhouse could not render appropriate care to lessen his fits of violence or to diminish the terrors of his illness. The master of the institution told Dix that if he could " 'take him out daily for exercise in the open air, it would do him good; but with the care of a farm, which he is expected and required to keep under profitable cultivation, with a family of paupers—often exceeding one hundred—to manage and provide for, he has not time to nurse madmen, or to give them in any degree the care they need.' " The inmate had homicidal tendencies: he terrified everyone but the master, whose only safety—as he thought—consisted in governing him through the *"principle of fear."*

The master gave Dix a chilling example of that principle. " 'Going to his room one day, not long since,' " the master related,

> in order to shave him, my hands both being full, as I came near, he suddenly sprang upon me, and dealt a violent blow at my chest; his being chained, alone prevented his killing me. I knew I must master him now or never; I threw down the shaving tools, caught a stick of wood from the entry, and laid upon him until he cried for quarter: I beat him long enough to make him know I was his master, and now he is too much afraid of a thrashing to attack me; but you had better stand off, ma'am, for he won't fear you.

In the basement of the Salem County Poorhouse, Dix encountered a feeble old man lying on a small bed. On asking

The New Jersey State Lunatic Asylum, 1849.

about his history, she was shocked to hear that this weak and depressed old man—"a pauper, helpless, lonely, and yet conscious of surrounding circumstances, and not now wholly oblivious of the past"—was a former judge and member of the New Jersey Legislature. He had lost his property through business reverses, had become violent, and had been committed to the county jail in chains "for greater security." Eventually his violence gave way to a calmer state, and he was moved to the poorhouse in which Dix saw him. She was struck that such a good citizen and pillar of the community, a victim of disease and misfortune, could be left to wither away in an obscure cell in a county poorhouse, receiving only a "share of that care and attention that must be divided and subdivided among the hundred feeble, infirm, and disabled inmates."

Visiting the Burlington County Poorhouse near Pemberton, Dix found twenty-two insane persons, ten of them occupants of the cells in the cellar or " 'low basement.' " She found these quarters to be "strange and woful [sic] contrast to the rooms above." The dreary confined cells of the low basement were "insufficiently lighted, insufficiently warmed, and pervaded the foul air to an intolerable degree." They truly offered a scene "at which humanity revolts."

It was not the facilities for the insane in Monmouth County's Shrewsbury Township that incensed Dix but the total lack of supervision in them. One "crazy man" had been allowed periodically to " 'wander into the woods, absenting himself till hunger forced his return.' " After appeasing his appetite, he would depart until one day " *'he did not come back at all.'* " That was in August 1844, three months before Dix learned of the incident. A local official told her that perhaps " 'he has gone home to friends—we lay out to write; we have talked of it for some time.' " Dix was outraged at the horror of "a feeble insane man gone *three months* from the watch of those who had, officially, the care of him" but who had neither made a diligent inquiry about him nor instituted a search.

Journeying northwest, Dix came to the township poorhouse in the Middlesex County community of North Brunswick. Here she saw a cell "occupied by a crazy man, who at times was subject to furious madness. He was chained and lying in a sort of box." So far as Dix could see, "this was a sort of narrow pen, made by nailing two boards of unequal length to the floor and partition; it contained some straw and sufficient coverings. The condition of the man was repulsive and filthy. . . ." She believed the superintendents of the poorhouse did their best to care for him but the task of changing his garments and washing and shaving him was difficult. There were times when it was considered impracticable. His cell, like those of the other inmates, measured only six feet by ten.

Also in Middlesex County, Dix visited the poorhouse in Piscataway Township. Here she found a violent man kept in a small wooden building located a few hundred yards from the principal dwelling. The structure's one room was "cold and damp, . . . bare of all furniture, dark and dull, and utterly comfortless." Its lone occupant was "chained, naked, except [for] a straight jacket laced so as to impede the motion of the arms, and hands. . . ." Exposed and filthy, he raged like "an imprisoned tiger" and often uttered "the foulest, vilest language." Sometimes, for a moment, he lapsed into quietness only to become again "like a demon writhing and raving." These circumstances presented Dix with "a scene utterly horrible and appalling." The mistress of the poorhouse readily admitted that she could " 'neither keep him clothed nor warmed: the stove is of no use [because of the danger of a fire], and he destroys at once whatever is put in for bedding, thrusting it through the opening in the floor.' " " 'He suffers dreadfully,' " she continued, " ' and sometimes we are afraid he will die in some terrible manner of cold, and wounds, and pain.' "

In North Jersey, conditions were no better. Essex County gave its municipalities sole authority for its insane. Some lunatics were kept in local poorhouses while others were " 'set off to the lowest bidder,' or those who agreed to take them for a given time, at the lowest rates." Newark had a poorhouse a short distance from the city. Here, Dix discovered a woman "who was kept in an outhouse in the yard. The room measured about nine feet by twelve, and nine high; it was lighted by a window, and *could* be ventilated by opening this, and the door. Neither was the room clean, nor the occupant."

Dix found the poorhouse in Paterson "poor in every sense." Located more than a mile from town, she deemed it "the most ill-ordered place . . . in the state of New Jersey." The structure was old and dilapidated, and it may have "received a coat of white-wash since it was first built, but this is conjectural. . . . The occupied rooms were positively loathsome." After her tour of the facility, Dix was in complete agreement with a Passaic County citizen who informed her that " 'our poor-house is wretched, and our poor are wretchedly managed. . . . The condition of the insane poor among us, and in New Jersey at large, has been a disgrace to a people claiming even the name of Christian.' "

At the Morris County Poorhouse in Hanover Township, Dix uncovered still further evidence of the horrible treatment of the state's insane. Here, she chanced on an area in the cellar that was used to imprison "violently excited maniacs." It contained two cells

> constructed of plank and boards. These dreary places were seven and a half feet high, by eight square; dark, damp, and unfurnished, unwarmed and unventilated—one would not hesitate, but [to] refuse to shut up a worthless dog . . . [there]; and so felt the master of the house and physician, who prefer *the alternative of chaining* the patients *clogs* and *fetters,* to the responsiblity and inhumanity of putting them into these savage dens. A small aperture cut at the end of one of these cells, some time ago occasioned the involuntary death of the crazy tenant, who thrusting his head through his eagerness to escape, could not withdraw it, and hanging there died. A female maniac died in the adjoining cell.

The master told Dix that " 'this . . . is not the place for crazy people; we have no means of properly controlling the outrageous, or of taking fit care of those who are more quiet.' " It was the opinion of the physician that New Jersey was in "need of a State Hospital."

Dix completed her fact-finding journey by touring Somerset and Mercer counties. In Somerset's Franklin Township Poorhouse, the mistress readily admitted " 'we have no fit place for crazy folks.' " No mentally ill were there at the time of Dix's visit but " *'strong chains had been sent,'* and a room prepared" for an insane woman who was expected soon. Trenton's poorhouse, located a few miles outside of New Jersey's capital city, was a fitting last stop.

This facility was small and "inconveniently constructed for separating or classifying the inmates." Dix encountered a mentally ill woman who was "lodged in an apartment on the second floor, entered by passing through the old men's sleeping room." In a bed next to hers, separated by a slight partition-screen, the New Englander found a helpless paralytic woman and her feeble husband. A third bed in the same room contained an infirm old man. Thus, three poor invalids were at the mercy of an "often furious and noisy mad-woman, who rends off her garments, and utters imprecations and obscene language that appal all within hearing." The mistress explained to Dix that " 'it is the only room we have to put her in. . . . We do not know what may happen among us any day; she may commit a murder, or burn the house; in short, we are in her power; but we do as well as we can; we are afraid to make her angry, and let her have her own will pretty much.' "

On January 23, 1845, Joseph S. Dodd, an Essex County Whig, introduced in the state senate a memorial Dix had written based on her recent survey.[45] Dix began by scolding the lawmakers for remaining "*behind* the age" in alleviating the sufferings of the insane. She warned that the number of incurables among the state's 610 mentally ill citizens was increasing "for want of appropriate remedial care."[46] She supported this assertion with her elaborate collection of horror stories from all over New Jersey.

Addressing herself to all the citizens of the state, Dix asked, "have you human feelings, can you delay this work which is solicited for the benefit of those who are . . . emphatically your wards, the wards of the state; for whose condition hereafter you are certainly accountable—inasmuch as you are largely able to provide a refuge . . . for the diseased, as their forlorn condition requires?"[47] Mental illness, she argued, is a curable disease, and a larger percentage of the persons it attacks are restored. The memorial closed with the contention that "on the ground of discreet economy alone, it is wise to establish a State Hospital in New Jersey." Dix noted that running an asylum would cost less than supporting the insane in numerous jails, poorhouses, and private families; it would save the state the many dollars lost each year through the "uncontrolled habits of destructiveness" of wandering insane persons; and it would eliminate the support of that "large class of incurables, who, if timely treated, would have been restored."[48]

Moved by the disinterested efforts and appeals of the determined reformer, the legislature appointed a bipartisan joint committee on February 11, 1845, to report on the expediency of erecting a lunatic asylum. A week earlier the Salem County Poorhouse, one of the places Dix visited, had burned to the ground. All of the inmates had been saved, but attention had focused on two insane paupers who had been rescued while chained in their cells. On February 25, the members of the committee presented their findings.[49]

The committeemen believed that "none in the department of philantropic effort prefers higher claims to our regard, or is more worthy the charity and munificence of the state" than the poor, degraded mentally disturbed. They praised the work of past committees for bringing the sufferings of the mentally ill to public attention and reminded their colleagues in the legislature that all of those committees had strongly advocated erecting an asylum "both on the ground of duty and economy." New Jersey was ready to begin and consummate such a project and could do so "without any additional tax, without feeling it to be a burden."[50]

One of the committeemen's most effective arguments in favor of an asylum, in view of the state's financial sensitivities, was that New Jersey could support its insane poor more cheaply "by an institution . . . than by the present method." They informed their fellow legislators that it was a medical fact that insanity in its early stages was curable. Referring to the records of mental institutions established in other states, they showed that a large proportion of recent cases recovered "when submitted to the remedial agency of a well-regulated asylum." However, New Jersey's practice of consigning its madmen to prisons and almshouses not only failed to restore individuals but also made their conditions worse until they were beyond the reach of medical aid. As a consequence, most of the state's insane continued for life as charges of the community. Convinced that it was not difficult to decide which of the two courses was more economical, the committeemen urged the legislature to "be up and doing" and to establish a state mental hospital.[51]

Yet, even after this strong confirmation of Dix's suggestion for an asylum the legislature obstinately refused to act. Some members could not agree to spend so much money on a "few lunatics," while others accused Dix and the joint committee of hyperbole.[52] One legislator, whom the press described as an "unterrified and unconverted Assemblyman," went so far as to deliver the follwing speech during the debate on the mental hospital in the lower house:

> Sir, I shall not trust the estimate of . . . [those] who have devised the plan of this Egyptain Collosheum [sic]. New Jersey has hitherto acted well. She has kept clear of a national debt, which some folks call a national blessing. Let us husband our resources. I had rather spend the money in educating the children of the State, . . . qualifying them to act their part well in life, and preparing them for eternity. . . . There'll be a day of account, and its not far ahead. . . . I do believe that if that Miss Dix had been paid $500 or $600, and escorted over the Delaware or to Philadelphia, or even $1,000 and taken to Washington City, and, if you choose, enshrined in the White House, it would have been money well laid out. Now, I should like the whys and wherefores for a building 487 feet long and 80 feet wide, for, maybe, twenty lunatics. I believe that the best thing we could do, would be to appropriate $200 or $300, to fill up the cellars [wherein the insane are kept] and sow them with grass-seed, so that . . . [such places] may not be seen hereafter. You couldn't do a more popular act![53]

At this point, Dix began her real work. Her previous efforts had merely supplemented the research and planning begun in 1839, but now she started to lobby day and night. She invited legislators to her rooms and overcame their objections and their reluctance to act.[54] In a letter to a friend in Philadelphia, she explained the process and an especially rewarding success:

> At Trenton, thus far, all is prosperous, but you cannot imagine the labor of conversing and convincing. Some evenings I had at once twenty gentlemen for three hours' steady conversation. The last evening, a rough country member, who had announced in the House that the 'wants of the insane of New Jersey were all

humbug,' and who came to overwhelm me with his arguments, after listening an hour and a half with wonderful patience to my details and to principles of treatment, suddenly moved into the middle of the parlor, and thus delivered himself: 'Ma'am, I bid you good-night! I do not want, for my part, to hear anything more; the others can stay if they want to. *I am convinced;* you've conquered me out and out; I shall vote for the hospital. If you'll come to the House, and talk there as you've done here, no man that isn't a brute can stand [against] you. . . . The Lord bless you!'—and thereupon he departed.[55]

Dix also worked through the press. She wrote numerous articles and encouraged others to do so. Newspapers throughout the state carried such items, as well as her memorial to the legislature. One man from Cape May was so moved by her ideas that he wrote to the *Trenton State Gazette* that "if the representatives of the people, after reading this memorial through, and contemplating the thrilling scenes therein depicted, do not feel a responsibility resting upon them, paramount to all pecuniary considerations, they must have hearts which cannot be touched by the *wailings of misery* or the *cry of distress.*"[56] Earlier, the editor of that paper had argued that "a Lunatic Asylum can be erected without the imposition of one additional cent of tax." In the northern part of the state, the readers of the *Newark Daily Advertiser* were told that either New Jersey must build a hospital for its insane or continue to use jails and poorhouses as the "receptacles of these miserable creatures." If the legislature did not act for the mentally ill, "chains and cells and an existence of hopeless misery" would continue "to be their portion."[57] Such publicity resulted in a flood of petitions to the legislature supporting the erection of a state asylum.[58]

On March 25, 1845, Dorothea Dix's remarkable display of personal force came to fruition when the legislature finally passed the bill to authorize the establishment of a state hospital. Senator Dodd sent her the following brief message to herald the event: "I am happy to announce to you the passage unanimously of the bill for the New Jersey State Lunatic Asylum."[59] The senate vote was 18-0, and the general assembly vote was 41-8.[60] In an editorial, the *Trenton State Gazette* happily called the asylum legislation "the most useful measure

... passed by the legislature of New Jersey for many years."[61]

Three years were to pass before the hospital opened on May 15, 1848, in Ewing Township near Trenton. The twenty-fourth mental institution to be established in the United States, it had a capacity of two hundred patients. Significantly, New Jersey was the last state in the Northeast to give the insane either public or private care on a statewide basis. Dix was particularly pleased with the new asylum because it was, as she later said, her "first-born child"—the first mental institution she was responsible for founding.[62]

In the decade that followed her crusade in New Jersey, she journeyed over thirty thousand miles. Such traveling in the mid-ninteenth century was an especially arduous ordeal. Roads were usually rough and often covered by mud. River travel on steamboats was never peaceful or free from incidents such as boiler explosions. On her journeys, Dix, in middle age and suffering from persistent lung trouble and chronic malaria, was constantly subjected to discomforts and accidents. But her remarkable faith and will sustained her. She visited hundreds of prisons, poorhouses, jails, and hospitals; collected data, prepared memorials, and aroused public opinion over the plight of the insane. Her appeals stimulated the legislatures of Pennsylvania, Indiana, Illinois, Kentucky, Tennessee, Missouri, Louisiana, Alabama, South Carolina, North Carolina, and Maryland to vote for supporting state hospitals and brought about the founding of the hospitals at Halifax, Nova Scotia and St. John, Newfoundland.[63]

During this peripatetic period, Dix attempted to alter radically the manner in which mental hospitals were financed —she solicited aid from the federal government. In 1848, she presented a memorial to Congress requesting a bill to distribute five million acres of federal land to the states to support the indigent insane. Precedents for such a subsidy existed in federal land grants for education and railroad construction. Numerous clergymen, prominent reformers, newspapermen, and government officials wrote or acted in support of her program.[64]

For the next six years, Dix labored in and out of congressional corridors to persuade the members of both houses that her project was not only desirable but also necessary. At

Dorothea Dix, undated oil by Thomas Waterman Wood (1823–1903). Original at Harrisburg (Pennsylvania) State Hospital.

first, she received little legislative backing. Congressmen were preoccupied with the intensifying sectional conflict that had become more bitter with the close of the Mexican War. Although her persistent lobbying eventually gained support for her bill, the 30th Congress adjourned on March 3, 1849, without passing it in either chamber.[65]

Dix resumed her struggle in 1850 when she presented the 31st Congress with a new bill asking for more than twelve million acres. It passed in the Senate but not in the House. A similar bill for a ten-million-acre appropriation passed in the House in 1852 during the 32nd Congress but failed in the Senate. Finally, both houses of the 34th Congress passed a bill early in 1854, setting aside ten million acres to be used by the states for the indigent insane. The jubilant reformer's triumph was of short duration, for President Franklin Pierce vetoed the bill on the grounds that it was unwise for the federal government to assume the support of the nation's poor and unconstitutional for it to make land grants for charitable purposes.[66] Dix's dream of removing sole responsibility for the care of the mentally ill from the states and localities was lost for the nineteenth century.

Staggered by defeat and exhausted by years of labor, Dix went abroad for a rest in 1854. Shortly after her arrival in Great Britain, she became interested in the condition of the insane in Scotland. She could not rest. After securing a lunacy commission for the Scots and instituting reforms in the Channel Islands, she set out on an extensive tour of the hospitals, prisons, and insane asylums of Europe. Her journey took her through fourteen countries and into hundreds of institutions.[67] When she returned to America in 1856, she was an international celebrity.

Dix spent the next four years in unremitting activity, traveling extensively, again helping to enlarge nearly all the institutions she had founded, as well as founding new ones.[68] Much of her work was in the South. Although as a Unitarian and a good New Englander she abominated slavery, Dix refused to mix her mission to the insane with the crusade against the peculiar institution. Thus, in these years before the Civil War, she was one of the few northern social activists who received a warm welcome in the southern states.[69]

When the war broke out, Dix volunteered her services to the federal government. In June of 1861, she was appointed superintendent of United States Army Nurses. Although not a nurse herself and lacking direct hospital experience, her unique career probably made her better acquainted with hospital organization than almost any person in the country. Throughout the entire war, she did not miss a day of work even though she became so ill for a time that she had to direct her activities from bed. In 1865, she was among the last to resign her responsibilities. When Edwin M. Stanton, the secretary of war, offered her various official honors, including a vote of money from Congress in return for her wartime service, she responded by asking for "the flag of my country."[70] On January 25, 1867, her request was granted.

With peace, she resumed her travels and continued her investigations, creating more new hospitals.[71] In 1881, Dix—always a sickly person—became very ill while visiting the Trenton State Hospital. Immediately, the staff invited her to be their honored guest for the remainder of her life. She had become an invalid, but she lived comfortably in a three-room apartment set aside for her in the hospital.[72] On the evening of July 18, 1887, the most famous and influential psychiatric reformer of the nineteenth century died at the age of eighty-five.

Dorothea Dix was responsible for founding or enlarging more than thirty mental hospitals in the United States and abroad. Although others often prepared the groundwork, she acted as a catalyst who brought various projects to fruition. Her most important contribution was to stimulate state government's role in providing institutional care and treatment for the mentally ill. Of course, Dix's work required a base of support. Such backing existed in most states in the form of groups committed to aiding the insane through the expansion of governmental activities. Creating and strengthening the formal institutions of state government was a dominant trend of the nineteenth century.[73] Dix's crusade for the institutional care of the insane, consequently, could take firm root in the minds of the American people.

Dr. Charles H. Nichols of the Bloomingdale Hospital in New York may well have written Dix's epitaph in a letter he sent to a friend in England: "There has died and been laid to rest in the most quiet, unostentatious way the most useful and distinguished woman America has yet produced."[74] Perhaps, however, her own words capture her spirit and her legacy even better: "Life is not to be expended in vain regrets. No day, no hour, comes but brings in its train works to be performed for some useful end,—the suffering to be comforted, the wandering led home, the sinner reclaimed. Oh! How can any fold the hands to rest, and say to the spirit, 'Take thine ease, for all is well'!"[75]

Notes

1. Gerald N. Grob, "Modernization and Traditionalism in Jacksonian Social Reform," in *Men, Women, and Issues in American History*, ed. Howard H. Quint and Milton Cantor (Homewood, Ill.: Dorsey Press, 1975), pp. 193-94, 197-98, 214; C. E. Black, *The Dynamics of Modernization* (New York: Harper and Row, 1966), pp. 1-26.
2. Helen E. Marshall, *Dorothea Dix: Forgotten Samaritan* (Chapel Hill: University of North Carolina Press, 1937), pp. 3, 5-6.
3. Ibid., p. 13; Seth Curtis Beach, *Daughters of the Puritans* (Freeport, N.Y.: Books for Libraries Press, 1967), p. 126.
4. Beach, *Daughters*, pp. 126-27.
5. *Calendar of Letters of Dorothea Lynde Dix, 1876-1885* (Newark: Historical Records Survey, 1941), p. 2: Marshall, *Forgotten Samaritan*, pp. 12, 14; Beach, *Daughters*, pp. 127-28.
6. Beach, *Daughters*, p. 129; Marshall, *Forgotten Samaritan*, pp. 16-17.
7. Marshall, *Forgotten Samaritan*, pp. 17, 22-23, 48; Beach, *Daughters*, pp. 129-30.
8. Grob, "Jacksonian Social Reform," p. 196; Marshall, *Forgotten Samaritan*, pp. 32-40.
9. Beach, *Daughters*, p. 132; Marshall, *Forgotten Samaritan*, pp. 21, 32, 48.
10. Marshall, *Forgotten Samaritan*, p. 51; Beach, *Daughters*, pp. 137-38; Francis Tiffany, *Life of Dorothea Lynde Dix* (Boston: Houghton Mifflin, 1891), p. 45.
11. Marshall, *Forgotten Samaritan*, pp. 54-55; Beach, *Daughters*, pp. 139-40.
12. Grob, "Jacksonian Social Reform," pp. 203-4; Marshall, *Forgotten Samaritan*, pp. 57, 60; Beach, *Daughters*, pp. 141-42.
13. Alice Felt Tyler, *Freedom's Ferment: Phases of American Social History* . . . (Minneapolis: University of Minnesota Press, 1944), pp. 304-5; Beach, *Daughters*, p. 142; Marshall, *Forgotten Samaritan*, p. 61.
14. Marshall, *Forgotten Samaritan*, pp. 61-62; Beach, *Daughters*, pp. 142-44; Tyler, *Freedom's Ferment*, p. 305.
15. Frederick M. Herrmann, "The Political Origins of the New Jersey State Insane Asylum, 1837-1860," in *Jacksonian New Jersey*, ed. Paul A. Stellhorn (Trenton: New Jersey Historical Commission, 1979), p. 85.
16. Marshall, *Forgotten Samaritan*, p. 63; U.S. Census Office, *Sixth Census of the United States, 1840* (Washington, D.C.: Department of State,

1841), p. 475; Gerald N. Grob, *Mental Institutions in America: Social Policy to 1875* (New York: Free Press, 1973), pp. 372-395. The total population for the United States in 1840 is given incorrectly in Marshall, *Forgotten Samaritan,* p. 63. The author cited the total population figure for 1850 by mistake.
17. Marshall, *Forgotten Samaritan,* pp. 63-64, 82.
18. Grob, "Jacksonian Social Reform," p. 204.
19. Tyler, *Freedom's Ferment,* p. 305.
20. Ibid., pp. 305-6; Grob, "Jacksonian Social Reform," pp. 204-5.
21. Marshall, *Forgotten Samaritan,* pp. 98-104; Margaret Joy Spalding, "Dorothea Dix and the Care of the Insane from 1841 to the Pierce Veto of 1854" (Ph.D. dissertation, Bryn Mawr College, 1976), pp. 90-93; Grob, *Mental Institutions,* n. 11, pp. 350-51. Grob argues that although Dix's biographers have given her credit for inducing Butler to support financially the establishment of the hospital, there is some evidence that indicates her efforts were not decisive.
22. Marshall, *Forgotten Samaritan,* p. 99; Spalding, "Dix," p. 94-96.
23. Beach, *Daughters,* p. 181; Tiffany, *Dix,* pp. 104-5; Grob, *Mental Institutions,* p. 355.
24. Joseph F. Mahoney, "The Impact of Industrialization on the New Jersey Legislature, 1870-1900: Some Preliminary Views," in *New Jersey Since 1860, New Findings and Interpretations,* ed. William C. Wright (Trenton: New Jersey Historical Commission, 1972), pp. 60-75; Frederick M. Herrmann, "Stress and Structure: Political Change in Antebellum New Jersey" (Ph.D. dissertation, Rutgers University, 1976), pp. 27-34; Grob, *Mental Institutions,* pp. 36-38; Ronald G. Walters, *American Reformers, 1815-1860* (New York: Hill and Wang, 1978), p. 3.
25. Gerald N. Grob, "The Political System and Social Policy in the Nineteenth Century: Legacy of the Revolution," *Mid-America* 58 (January 1976): 11-12, 16; Grob, *Mental Institutions,* pp. 271-72; Grob, *Edward Jarvis and the Medical World of Nineteenth-Century America* (Knoxville: University of Tennessee Press, 1978) pp. 109-10.
26. Grob, "Political System," pp. 6-7; Frank J. Esposito, "New Jersey's Identity Crisis," in *The Outlook on New Jersey,* ed. Silvio R. Laccetti (Union City, N.J.: Wm. H. Wise, 1979), p. 12.
27. *Votes and Proceedings of the . . . General Assembly of the State of New Jersey . . . ,* 1841, p. 19 (hereafter cited as *General Assembly*); "Report Relative to an Asylum for Lunatics," *General Assembly,* 1841, pp. 521-533; Herrmann, "Stress and Structure," pp. 271-72; *Journal of the Proceedings of the Legislative Council of the State of New Jersey . . . ,* 1839, p. 268 (hereafter cited as *Legislative Council*).
28. Grob, *Mental Institutions,* pp. 12-13, 35-38, 108; Edward Jarvis, *Insanity and Idiocy in Massachusetts: Report of the Commission on Lunacy, 1855,* with an introduction by Gerald N. Grob (Cambridge: Harvard University Press, 1971), pp. 5, 7, 18, 28; Paul T. Stafford, *Government and the Needy: A Study of Public Assistance in New Jersey* (Princeton: Princeton University Press, 1941), p. 7.
29. Horace A. Buttolph, *Historical and Descriptive Account of the New Jersey State Lunatic Asylum at Trenton* (Trenton: n.p., 1849), p. 1; James Leiby, *Charity and Correction in New Jersey: A History of State*

Welfare Institutions (New Brunswick: Rutgers University Press, 1967), p. 49; David L. Cowen, *Medicine and Health in New Jersey: A History* (Princeton: D. Van Nostrand, 1964), p. 102.
30. *Legislative Council,* 1839, pp. 267–68.
31. Ibid., pp. 268–69.
32. Ibid., p. 272.
33. Leiby, *Charity and Correction,* pp. 49–50; *General Assembly,* 1840, pp. 444–47.
34. *General Assembly,* 1840, p. 449.
35. Ibid., p. 450.
36. Ibid., pp. 451, 453.
37. *Legislative Council,* 1841, pp. 223–24, 232.
38. Ibid., pp. 232–33. The committee's cost estimate was very accurate; between 1848 and 1860 the state appropriated an average of $15,942 per year for its mental institution. See Herrmann, "Stress and Structure," n. 56, p. 317.
39. *Legislative Council,* 1841, p. 234.
40. *Legislative Council,* 1842, p. 167.
41. *New Jersey Laws,* P.L. 1843, pp. 82–83.
42. *General Assembly,* 1845, pp. 492–93.
43. Tyler, *Freedom's Ferment,* pp. 304–6; Grob, *Mental Institutions,* p. 356; Francis Bazley Lee, *New Jersey as a Colony and as a State . . . ,* 4 vols. (New York: Publishing Society of New Jersey, 1902), 3:293–94; Buttolph, *Lunatic Asylum,* p. 2; Leiby, *Charity and Correction,* pp. 50–51.
44. Dix's experiences are recounted in her memorial, which is printed in the *Journal of the Proceedings of the . . . Senate of the State of New Jersey,* 1845, pp. 176–97 (hereafter cited as *Senate*).
45. *Newark Daily Advertiser,* January 24, 1845.
46. *Senate,* 1845, p. 177.
47. Ibid., p. 198.
48. Ibid., pp. 207–8, 210, 214.
49. Ibid., p. 327; Marshall, *Forgotten Samaritan,* p. 105; Joseph Sickler, *Dorothea Dix in New Jersey* (n.p.: n.p., n.d.), p. 6; Cowen *Medicine and Health,* p. 103; *General Assembly,* 1845, pp. 491–96. *Newark Daily Advertiser,* October 10, 1844, gave the political affiliations of the 1845 legislature.
50. *General Assembly,* 1845, pp. 492–93, 495.
51. Ibid., pp. 495–96.
52. Cowen, *Medicine and Health,* p. 103.
53. Tiffany, *Dix,* pp. 115–16.
54. Cowen, *Medicine and Health,* p. 103; Leiby, *Charity and Correction,* p. 51.
55. Tiffany, *Dix,* pp. 114–15; Marshall, *Forgotten Samaritan,* p. 107.
56. Tiffany, *Dix,* pp. 109–10; Sickler, *Dix,* pp. 11–12; *Newark Daily Advertiser,* February 18, 1845; February 19, 1845; *Trenton State Gazette,* January 31, 1845; February 26, 1845.
57. *Trenton State Gazette,* January 29, 1845; *Newark Daily Advertiser,* February 19, 1845.
58. *Trenton State Gazette,* March 14, 1845; March 17, 1845; *Senate,* 1845,

pp. 230, 485, 567, 604, 626; *General Assembly,* 1845, pp. 554, 607, 625, 631, 643.
59. Tiffany, *Dix,* p. 118; Marshall, *Forgotten Samaritan,* p. 107.
60. *Senate,* 1845, pp. 632, 701; *General Assembly,* 1845, p. 661. The asylum act was signed by the governor on March 26, 1845; see *New Jersey Laws,* P.L. 1845, pp. 164–65.
61. *Trenton State Gazette,* March 21, 1845.
62. Lee, *New Jersey,* p. 294; U.S. Census Office, *Eighth Census of the United States, 1860, Population* (Washington, D.C.: Department of State, 1864), pp. xcvii–xcviii; Leiby, *Charity and Correction,* p. 56; Grob, *Mental Institutions,* pp. 374–395; Herrmann, "Political Origins," p. 92; Tiffany, *Dix,* p. 105; Marshall, *Forgotten Samaritan,* p. 108
63. Tyler, *Freedom's Ferment,* p. 306; Tiffany, *Dix,* pp. 124, 127–30, 134; Marshall, *Forgotten Samaritan,* p. 114; Beach, *Daughters,* pp. 154–56; Grob, *Mental Institutions,* p. 354.
64. Grob, *Mental Institutions,* p. 200; Tyler, *Freedom's Ferment,* p. 306; Walter I. Trattner, *From Poor Law to Welfare State: A History of Social Welfare in America* (New York: Free Press, 1974), p. 61.
65. Grob, *Mental Institutions,* p. 200; Trattner, *Poor Law to Welfare State,* p. 62; Spalding, "Dix," p. 137.
66. Grob, *Mental Institutions,* pp. 200–1; Spalding, "Dix," pp. 145, 154–55, 164–66, 171, 183, 190, 192; Tyler, *Freedom's Ferment,* pp. 306–7; James D. Richardson, *A Compilation of the Messages and Papers of the Presidents, 1789–1897,* 10 vols. (Washington, D.C.: Government Printing Office, 1897), 5:247–56. Dix's years of federal lobbying did not completely meet with failure. In 1855, due to her efforts, Congress enacted legislation that established the Government Hospital for the Insane (later St. Elizabeth's Hospital) in Washington, D.C.; see Grob, *Mental Institutions,* pp. 201, 395; Marshall, *Forgotten Samaritan,* pp. 146–47, 241; Beach, *Daughters,* p. 157.
67. Tyler, *Freedom's Ferment,* p. 307; Marshall, *Forgotten Samaritan,* pp. 162, 174, 183.
68. *Calendar of Letters,* p. 5.
69. Marshall, *Forgotten Samaritan,* p. 192; Grob, *Mental Institutions,* p. 108.
70. Margaret Leech, *Reveille in Washington, 1860–1865* (New York: Harper and Brothers, 1941), pp. 209, 211; Marshall, *Forgotten Samaritan,* pp. 202, 206–7, 210, 230–31.
71. Marshall, *Forgotten Samaritan,* pp. 235–36.
72. William John Ellis, "New Jersey's Florence Nightingale," *Towpath* 1 (November 1940): 8.
73. Grob, "Jacksonian Social Reform," p. 205; Marshall, *Forgotten Samaritan,* p. 245; Herrmann, "Stress and Structure," pp. 2, 263–64, 311, 342–44, 349, 351.
74. Grob, *Mental Institutions,* pp. 247, 449; Tyler, *Freedom's Ferment,* p. 307; Marshall, *Forgotten Samaritan,* p. vii; Tiffany, *Dix,* p. 375.
75. Tiffany, *Dix,* p. 52; Marshall, *Forgotten Samaritan,* pp. 56–57.

For Further Reading

Dorothea L. Dix has had numerous biographers. Two of the best treatments of her life are Francis Tiffany, *Life of Dorothea Lynde Dix* (Boston: Houghton Mifflin Co., 1891) and Helen E. Marshall, *Dorothea Dix: Forgotten Samaritan* (Chapel Hill: University of North Carolina Press, 1937). Corinne Lowe, *The Gentle Warrior: A Study of Dorothea Lynde Dix* (New York: Harcourt, Brace, 1948) and Dorothy Clarke Wilson, *Stranger and Traveler: The Story of Dorothea Dix, American Reformer* (Boston: Little, Brown, 1975) are good popular studies of Dix's career. Brief, competent biographies of Dix appear in Gladys Brooks, *Three Wise Virgins* (New York: Dutton, 1957) and Seth Curtis Beach, *Daughters of the Puritans* (Freeport, N.Y.: Books for Libraries Press, 1967). More specific studies of her work are William John Ellis, "New Jersey's Florence Nightingale," *Towpath* 1 (November 1940): 6–17; Joseph Sickler, *Dorothea Dix in New Jersey* (n.p.: n.p., n.d.); and Margaret Joy Spalding, "Dorothea Dix and the Care of the Insane from 1841 to the Pierce Veto of 1854" (Ph.D. dissertation, Bryn Mawr College, 1976). Margaret Leech, *Reveille in Washington, 1860–1865* (New York: Harper and Brothers, 1941) covers Dix's contributions during the Civil War.

A number of works place Dix's achievements in a broad historical perspective. Alice Felt Tyler, *Freedom's Ferment: Phases of American Social History* . . . (Minneapolis: University of Minnesota Press, 1944), a classic work, sweepingly surveys antebellum social reform, while Walter I. Trattner, *From Poor Law to Welfare State: A History of Social Welfare in America* (New York: Free Press, 1974) synthesizes social welfare policies and practices from colonial times to the present. Nineteenth-century ideas about insanity and public policy toward the insane are discussed in Norman Dain, *Concepts of Insanity in the United States 1789-1865* (New Brunswick: Rutgers University Press, 1964); Gerald N. Grob, *Mental Institutions in America: Social Policy to 1875* (New York: Free Press, 1973); and Gerald N. Grob, *Edward Jarvis and the Medical World of Nineteenth-Century America* (Knoxville: University of Tennessee Press, 1978). David J. Rothman, *The Discovery of the Asylum: Social Order and Disorder in the New Republic* (Boston: Little, Brown, 1971), is a highly imaginative interpretation of reformatory institutions.

Various New Jersey histories provide an excellent starting point for studying Dix's role in founding the Garden State's first mental hospital. Paul T. Stafford, *Government and the Needy: A Study of Public Assistance in New Jersey* (Princeton: Princeton University Press, 1941); David L. Cowen, *Medicine and Health in New Jersey: A History* (Princeton: D. Van Nostrand, 1964); and James Leiby, *Charity and Correction in New Jersey: A History of State Welfare Institutions* (New Brunswick: Rutgers University Press, 1967) survey aspects of social history that provide a context for Dix's reform efforts. Two studies of the asylum itself are Horace A. Buttolph, *Historical and Descriptive Account of the New Jersey State Lunatic Asylum at Trenton* (Trenton: n.p., 1849) and Frederick M. Herrmann, "The Political Origins of the New Jersey State Insane Asylum, 1837-1860," in *Jacksonian New Jersey*, ed. Paul A. Stellhorn (Trenton: New Jersey Historical Commission, 1979). A chapter on social legislation in Peter D. Levine, *The Behavior of State Legislative Parties in the Jacksonian Era, New Jersey, 1829-1844* (Cranbury: Fairleigh Dickinson University Press, 1977) clarifies the politics behind Dix's work.

The Industrial Revolution had a profound impact on nineteenth-century social reform and its leaders such as Dix. C.E. Black, *The Dynamics of Modernization* (New York: Harper and Row, 1966) outlines the process of change caused by industrialization. Gerald N. Grob traces the effects of the rise of an urban-industrial society on politics and social reform in "Modernization and Traditionalism in Jacksonian Social Reform," in *Men, Women, and Issues in American History,* ed. Howard H. Quint and Milton Cantor (Homewood, Ill.: Dorsey Press, 1975), and in "The Political System and Social Policy in the Nineteenth Century: Legacy of the Revolution," *Mid-America* 58 (January 1976): 5-19. According to Ronald G. Walters, *American Reformers, 1815-1860* (New York: Hill and Wang, 1978), the modernization of American life in the years after 1815 was the basic force behind antebellum reforms. Frederick M. Herrmann, "Stress and Structure: Political Change in Antebellum New Jersey" (Ph.D. dissertation, Rutgers University, 1976) studies the relationship of rapid socio-economic changes to public policy decisions in the Garden State.

Various primary sources provide valuable information about Dix and her New Jersey activities. The *Pamphlet Laws of New Jersey* contain a legislative history of the origins of the mental hospital founded at Trenton. Investigatory committee reports are printed in the *Legislative Council (Senate) Journal* and the *Minutes of the General Assembly. A Memorial to the Senate and General Assembly Relative to the Care of Idiots, Epileptics and the Insane Poor of the State* is a basic document. Newspapers of the period such as the *Newark Daily Advertiser* and the *Trenton State Gazette* are essential too. Readers who wish to sample Dix's correspondence should consult *Calendar of Letters of Dorothea Lynde Dix, 1876-1885* (Newark: Historical Records Survey, 1941) and Charles M. Snyder, *The Lady and the President: The Letters of Dorothea Dix and Millard Fillmore* (Lexington: University Press of Kentucky, 1975).